PICTUREPEDIA

NOTE TO PARENTS

This book is part of PICTUREPEDIA, a completely
new kind of information series for children.
Its unique combination of pictures and words
encourages children to use their eyes to discover and
explore the world, while introducing them to a wealth
of basic knowledge. Clear, straightforward text
explains each picture thoroughly and provides
additional information about the topic.

"Looking it up" becomes an easy task with
PICTUREPEDIA, an ideal first reference for all types of
schoolwork. Because PICTUREPEDIA is also entertaining,
children will enjoy reading its words and looking
at its pictures over and over again. You can encourage
and stimulate further inquiry by helping your child
pose simple questions for the whole family to
"look up" and answer together.

JUNGLE
ANIMALS

A DK PUBLISHING BOOK

Consultant Dr. Mark Collins

Editor Deborah Chancellor
Art Editor Andrew Walker

US Editor B. Alison Weir

Series Editor Sarah Phillips
Series Art Editor Paul Wilkinson

Picture Researcher Paul Snelgrove
Photography Organizer Alison Verity

Production Manager Ian Paton

Editorial Director Jonathan Reed
Design Director Ed Day

First American Edition, 1992
10 9 8
Published in the United States by
DK Publishing Inc., 95 Madison Avenue
New York, New York 10016

Copyright © 1992 Dorling Kindersley Limited, London.
Visit us on the World Wide Web at
http://www.dk.com

Library of Congress Cataloging-in-Publication Data

Jungle animals / Mark Collins, editor. – 1st American ed.
    p. cm. – (Picturepedia)
    Includes index.
    Summary: Depicts and describes such jungle animals as fruit-eating
birds, bats, and big cats.
    ISBN 1-56458-139-X
    1. Jungle fauna – Encyclopedias, Juvenile. [1. Jungle animals.]
I. Collins. N. Mark. II. Series.
QL112.J86 1992
591.909'52 – dc20   92-52835
                                                              CIP
                                                              AC

Reproduced by Colourscan, Singapore
Printed and bound in Italy by Graphicom

JUNGLE ANIMALS

CONTENTS

JUNGLE LIFE

Imagine a place where there are more kinds of mammals, insects, birds, and plants than anywhere else in the world. You are surrounded by trees, and it is the hottest, stickiest, and wettest place on Earth. It is noisy, damp, and dark on the ground, but if you climb to the treetops, there is blazing sunlight. Where are you? You are in the jungle! Let's explore a jungle in South America.

An iguana catches insects in the leafy branches of jungle trees.

The heat is scorching up in the tall, flowering treetops. Heavy rain often pours and, sometimes, hurricanes howl.

Playful giant otters swim in jungle rivers, feeding on small river fish, mammals, and birds.

From the riverbank, the jungle looks much thicker than it really is. A wide wall of light-loving plants crowds in by the riverbank.

Lurking lazily by the riverbank is a dangerous caiman.

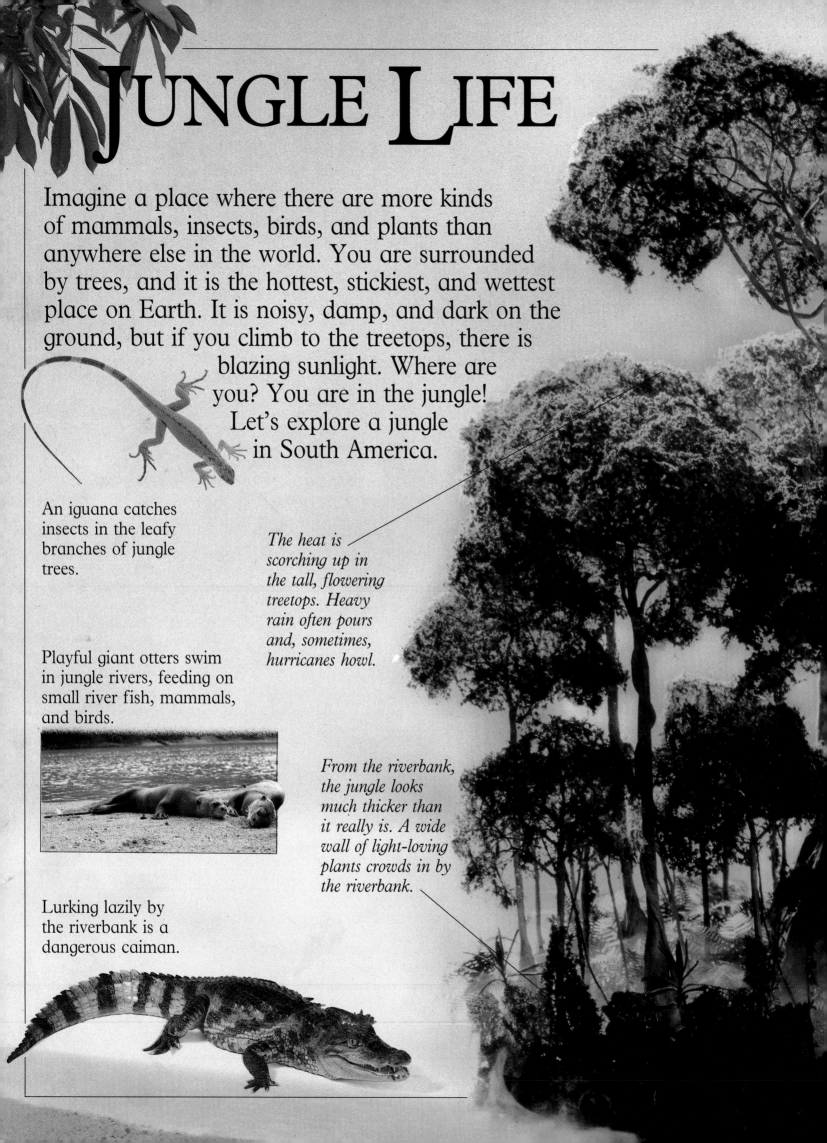

The tallest trees are called emergent trees.

A scarlet macaw eats fruit and spreads the seeds so that new trees can grow.

Many jungle plants have leaves that point downward, so the rain drips off them.

A bird's-eye view of the jungle is a beautiful sight. The canopy of trees stretches out like a huge, green carpet.

This howler monkey swings through the trees, eating the leaves and fruit.

A golden tree boa waits in the trees to snatch the next bird or bat that flies by.

There are about 25,000 kinds of orchids. Many grow on tree trunks in the jungle.

This morpho butterfly carries pollen between flowers, helping to make new seeds.

Woody vines, called lianas, trail down the tree trunks.

Only about two percent of the treetop sunlight reaches the dark, hot, and sticky jungle floor.

Huge, thick roots keep the tree trunks steady.

An ocelot sleeps during the day and hunts small animals at night.

ANIMAL FAMILIES

Do you have any relatives who live on the other side of the world? Some kinds of jungle animals are found only in one jungle. But animals in the same family, with similar hunting and eating habits, often can be found in another jungle thousands of miles away. There are three main areas of jungle – in South America, in Africa, and in Southeast Asia.

Spider monkey
(South America)

Big Cats
Jaguars, leopards, and clouded leopards are very similar. But they all hunt in different parts of the world.

Jaguar *(South America)*

Gorilla
(Africa)

Apes and Monkeys
The spider monkey, gorilla, and orangutan climb trees in different jungles. But they have never encountered one another in the wild.

Orangutan
(Southeast Asia)

All Joined Up
Millions of years ago, all the world's jungles were joined together in one big area of land, called Pangaea.

Moving Apart
Slowly, the Earth's crust moved. The huge continent broke apart and animals moved with the land. Today, many unrelated jungle animals live far apart, but they look alike and behave in similar ways.

In South America is the world's largest and wettest jungle!

In Africa is the jungle with the smallest number of plant species.

In Southeast Asia is the most mountainous jungle.

Clouded leopard *(Southeast Asia)*

White-cheeked turaco *(Africa)*

Rhinoceros hornbill *(Southeast Asia)*

Leopard *(Africa)*

Saffron toucanet *(South America)*

Fruit-eating Birds
The toucan, hornbill, and turaco all eat fruit and help spread seeds. They have the same job in different jungles.

PLANTS

Many jungle plants and animals can't live without each other. Countless animals could not survive without the food and shelter that jungle trees and other plants give them. Many jungle plants would die out, too, if animals didn't spread their pollen and seeds for them. Some plants even eat jungle animals to stay alive!

Mini Jungle

A pool of water collects in the middle of a bromeliad plant. Frogs lay eggs in the water, and many birds and lizards come by to catch the insects living there.

Bird-of-paradise flower

In just a few months, a pitcher plant can catch thousands of insects in its deep traps.

Flower Farmer

Many bats help grow their own food! They eat the sweet nectar of jungle plants, spreading pollen from flower to flower as they feed. This means that new plants can grow.

Watch Your Step!

If you think a jungle plant couldn't harm a fly, look at this monkey cup pitcher plant! If insects land on the rim, they skid and fall down inside the trap. Then they drown in a pool of sticky liquid at the bottom.

Traps grow at the end of a pitcher plant's leaves.

Urn plant

Ghost Story

A bird drops a strangling fig seed onto a tree's branches. In time, fig roots grow downward, surrounding the tree's trunk. Fig leaves soon block out the tree's light, and it dies. Then the strangler stands alone, like a ghost of the tree.

A lid keeps the rain out of each trap.

Leaf

Slippery rim

Insects drowned in the pool are broken down by strong chemicals made by the plant.

11

FRUIT-EATING BIRDS

In a flash of brilliant color, a flock of parrots suddenly takes off from the branches of a jungle fruit tree. Fruit trees grow from tiny seeds, and fruit-eating birds help spread fruit seeds, enabling new trees to take root and grow. But parrots are not the only colorful jungle birds that like wild fruit and nuts. Toucans and hornbills are just some of the many other jungle fruit-eaters.

Keel-billed Toucan
No one knows why toucans have such big beaks. Perhaps the bright colors help them tell each other apart.

Beak Parade

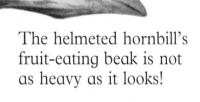

The helmeted hornbill's fruit-eating beak is not as heavy as it looks!

Tasty Fruit
This scarlet macaw has only 400 taste buds on its tongue, while humans have 9,000 taste buds. The macaw uses its tongue to taste if fruit is ripe.

This emerald-billed toucanet picks fruit carefully with its huge, colorful beak.

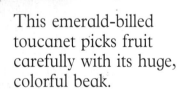

St. Vincent parrots have sharp, hooked beaks to tear open fruit.

Apple Bobbing
Try eating an apple without using your hands. It's not easy! Parrots solve this problem by holding fruit with their claws.

Up, Up, and Away!
Parakeets are members of the parrot family. Many of them live in the jungle and eat fruit. This is a canary-winged parakeet.

The parakeet uses its good eyesight to judge distances between the jungle trees.

A parakeet's short wings help it change direction quickly as it flies through the forest.

It needs strong wing muscles to flap its wings fast.

Even the brightest feathers can be hidden in the strong sunlight and dark shade of the leafy jungle treetops.

You can teach some pet parrots to "speak," but parrots don't imitate sounds in the wild.

Its claws hang down as it flies along, ready to grasp a branch when it lands in a tree.

Fruits of the Jungle
This rambutan fruit is a jungle favorite, along with wild figs, wild palms, and avocados.

Feeding the Family
A hornbill mother lays her eggs inside a hollow tree trunk and is sealed in with her chicks as they grow. Her mate feeds them all with fruit. Soon the nest is too small to hold her and the growing family, so she breaks her way out. Then both parents feed the chicks until they leave the nest.

13

NECTAR-EATING BIRDS

Erythrina plant from South America

Some jungle birds like to lap up nectar, the sweet liquid that is hidden deep inside a flower. Nectar is rich in water, vitamins, minerals, and, above all, sugar. The tiny hummingbirds of North and South America, and the sunbirds of Africa and Southeast Asia need to drink lots of nectar to build up enough energy to fly. Some eat more than half their weight in nectar every day.

Olive-backed sunbird

The petals are the same length as the nectar-eater's beak.

Sky Diver
A small hummingbird can flap its wings up to 70 times a second. It can twist and turn in midair, fly backward, and even upside down!

Sweet Tooth
Nectar is one-quarter sugar, and eating sugar gives you energy. You are bigger than a hummingbird and use up much more energy. You would need to eat 299 jars of honey every day if you were as active as a hummingbird.

Steady Perch
Like a hummingbird, this crimson sunbird has a long beak, bright feathers, and flies very fast. It usually perches on a flower to reach the nectar.

Nectar Seeker
The violet-cheeked hummingbird spends most of its time searching for nectar in the South American jungle.

Hummingbirds can see bright colors, and often fly to red flowers, such as this hibiscus.

Its beak is just the right length to reach deep inside a flower to feed on the nectar.

Light reflects on its bright feathers.

Strong wing muscles make up a third of the hummingbird's body weight.

Its feathers are closely packed together. This bird has about 1,000 feathers.

When a hummingbird is hovering, its heart beats very fast – about 1,260 times a minute!

Its chest will be dusted with pollen, which it will carry to the next flower it visits. This means that pollination can take place.

A hummingbird uses its small legs and feet for perching, not for walking or hopping.

Nest Egg
Female calliope hummingbirds build small nests high up in trees. They lay very tiny eggs and keep them warm until they hatch. The chicks are fed for about a month before they leave the nest.

(Actual size)

15

BATS

Bats are the only mammals in the world that can fly. A quarter of the world's mammals are bats, and if you added up all the different kinds of mammals in the jungle, more than half of them would be bats. If there are so many bats around, why are they so hard to spot? Most bats fly at night, hunting for food. They sleep hidden in trees during the day.

Its wings are muscle covered by skin.

Hanging Out
Bats can hang upside down for hours. During the day, hundreds of fruit bats roost together in jungle trees.

One finger sticks out like a claw and can be used for holding on to fruit.

Fish Fright
This fisherman bat swoops close to jungle rivers to snatch up fish with its huge, upturned claws.

Funny Faces
Bats have some of the funniest faces in the jungle. There are lots of different shapes and sizes.

Hammerheaded bat

Each foot has five claws that grip tightly onto branches.

Baby Boom
Fruit bats have only one baby at a time. A baby fruit bat is carried by its mother for eight weeks after it is born, then it learns to fly.

Borneo Fruit Bat

Its body is furry.

It has a foxlike face.

Its good eyesight and sense of smell help it find fruit.

Five fingers stretch out between its wings.

Finding Food
Some bats eat fruit, nectar, fish, and even blood, but most bats eat insects. Here's how a bat uses its hearing to find insects in the dark:

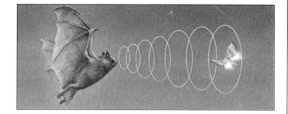

The bat sends out up to 200 squeaks a second. The squeaks are too high in pitch for people to hear.

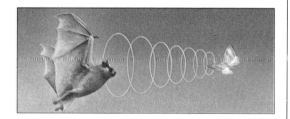

The squeaks hit insects and bounce back. This echo tells the bat where the insect is located.

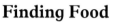

The bat then chases the insect and snatches it up. All this can happen in less than half a second.

Tent-building bat

Tube-nosed bat

Philippine horseshoe bat

GLIDING HIGH

When you throw a paper plane, air catches under the wings and, if you're lucky, it glides a long way. Some treetop animals have found a very clever, quick, and safe way of getting around in the jungle. They don't swing between the trees like monkeys or fly like birds and bats. Instead, they spread out special skin flaps and take off from the branches, gliding through the air like paper planes.

It uncoils quickly to take off from a branch.

Climbing up trees is made easier because of the rough scales on the snake's belly.

Stretch and Jump

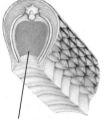

When this snake is resting in the trees, its body is shaped like a hose.

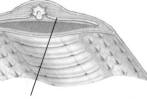

The snake stretches its ribs out and flattens its body when it is gliding.

Rock-a-bye Baby

This Philippine colugo needs a rest! She carries her baby as she glides between the trees. The furry flaps that stretch out when she glides are now being used as a cozy hammock for her baby.

Snake in the Sky

A paradise tree snake can glide 50 yards through the air. It does this to escape from hungry hawks and eagles.

Lizards, birds, frogs, and bats are gulped down head first.

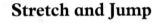

In the air, it moves its body in an S-shape to steer.

Sugar Seeker
Sugar gliders live in Australia and eat the sweet juice, called sap, of eucalyptus trees.

If the gap between two trees is too big to jump across, a sugar glider leaps off and glides to the closest branch.

Flying Frog
A flying frog takes off to escape from an enemy. It stretches out its webbed feet to glide through the air.

In mid-flight, the sugar glider spreads out its legs to balance. This stretches out its furry flaps.

The sugar glider jerks its bushy tail upward to slow down before landing on all fours on a tree trunk.

Air catches under the flying gecko's webbed feet, keeping it high in the sky.

Whizzing Lizard
An adult flying gecko uses its strong back legs to spring off from a branch. It can glide up to 18 yards between two trees.

As it glides, the flaps of skin around the gecko's belly spread out to trap the air.

APES

Are you good at swinging on a jungle gym? Imagine how much better you would be with an ape's strong arms and legs! Twenty million years ago, people had something like an ape's body. But since then, both apes and humans have changed a lot. Even today, apes are our closest animal relatives. We are both in the same group of animals, called primates.

Chimpanzees' thumbs are opposable. This means they can easily fold across the palm of the hand.

A lar gibbon swings between branches that are up to 40 feet (13 m) apart.

It has a big brain and is one of the world's most intelligent animals.

A chimpanzee can't cry tears, but it does have emotions. It can be angry, frightened, happy, or sad.

Rulers of the Jungle
The apes that live in the jungle are some of the strongest, most intelligent animals in the world.

Strong legs and arms help the chimpanzee climb up and down the tall jungle trees.

A chimpanzee usually moves around on all fours on the jungle floor.

Orangutan

Siamang gibbon

Pygmy chimpanzee

A gibbon lets go with both hands to swing between branches.

It swings forward by "rowing" the air with its legs.

Speedy Swinger
The champion acrobats of the animal kingdom are the small gibbons from Southeast Asia. They are the fastest primates in the world, and can swing through the trees at up to 20 miles (32 km) per hour.

Chimpanzees can use 19 different tools for finding and eating food. The only animal to use more tools is the human being.

Baby chimpanzees hear well with their big ears.

Intelligence Test
This chimpanzee is using a stick to trick tasty termites out of their nest. If it used its fingers instead, the termites would bite them.

Gentle Giant
Gorillas will fight only if one of their family is in danger. Sitting in peace on the jungle floor, they talk to each other using more than 22 different sounds. They have been heard to huff and puff, hiccup, yawn, and even burp!

Gorilla

Chimpanzee

Lar gibbon

MONKEYS

Woolly Coat
A woolly spider monkey has a thick coat like a teddy bear.

Just like humans, monkeys live in family groups. Most sleep at night and are wide awake during the day. Many South American monkeys have prehensile tails that can wind around branches in a tight grip. Monkeys in Africa and Southeast Asia do not have prehensile tails, but many of them are still amazing acrobats, spending most of their lives in the trees.

Common Marmoset
Marmosets live in South American jungles and are no bigger than squirrels. They jump between the trees to get around.

It holds food in its hands to eat. Fruit and nuts are often pinched and sniffed before being eaten.

Long arms and legs help it move quickly. It swings through trees as fast as a person can jog along the jungle floor below.

Spider Monkey
When spider monkeys feel threatened, they scratch their fur and bark like dogs. Eagles and jaguars hunt them in the jungle trees.

Its prehensile tail is much longer than its arms and thicker than its legs. The tail winds tightly around a branch to stop the monkey from falling out of the tree.

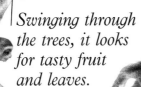

Swinging through the trees, it looks for tasty fruit and leaves.

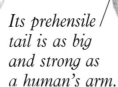

Its prehensile tail is as big and strong as a human's arm.

Monkey Faces

These colorful monkeys belong to the guenon family. They all live in Africa.

De Brazza's monkey

A Monkey's Tail

This squirrel monkey can hang from a branch while it eats. Monkeys that have prehensile tails like this are only found in South America.

Morning Call

Early in the morning, the howler monkey makes a very loud, booming sound. It is warning other animals to keep away, and telling other howler monkeys it is breakfast time.

Moustached monkey

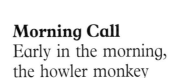

Diana monkey

Male   *Female and young*   *Male*

On the Move

Howler monkeys march along branches in single file. A big male leads and a small male follows at the rear.

White-nosed monkey

AWAKE AT NIGHT

Jungles are not like zoos – they do not close down at night. When it gets dark in the jungle, only some of the animals go to sleep. Others are just waking up and are hungry for something to eat. Animals that are awake at night are nocturnal. Many small jungle animals are nocturnal because there is less danger around for them at night.

Grab a Snack
At night, an African potto snatches insects with both hands and eats them with leaves and fruit. The spikes on its neck protect it if an enemy attacks.

A loris needs a thick coat of fur to keep warm at night. It would freeze without it.

What Big Eyes You Have!
A tarsier's eyes are so big that they take up most of its face. If your eyes were this huge, they would be the size of grapefruits.

Get a Grip
Many nocturnal animals live in trees. Their front paws are good at grasping branches.

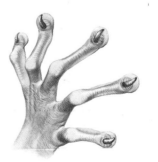

Tarsier

Loris

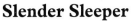

Slender Sleeper

During the day, this loris sleeps in the trees. It is called a slender loris because it has long, thin arms and legs.

A loris can see well in the dark with such big, round eyes.

A good sense of smell helps a loris find its way around at night.

Just like you, a loris has an opposable thumb that can be used to grip branches.

Lazy Bones

Sloths are awake at night, but they move so slowly that they look as if they are asleep! They carry their babies and eat while hanging upside down in trees.

A loris's feet are so good at holding on to branches, that it can hang from one leg as it feeds.

Aye-aye   Two-toed sloth

Midnight Feast

During the day, a rare aye-aye sleeps in a nest in the trees. It spends the night digging insects out of tree bark with its long third finger. To find out where the insects are, it has to listen carefully with its big ears.

BUTTERFLIES AND MOTHS

Did you know that butterflies and moths live in the jungle, too? Some are as large as your hand or as small as your thumbnail. Some have clever ways to protect themselves. Some taste so nasty that birds leave them alone. And some are so well camouflaged that birds never even see them!

The flame butterfly from South America likes to settle and lay its eggs on a passion flower plant.

A caterpillar has already chewed a hole in this leaf!

Copy Cats
These butterflies look the same, but the bottom one tastes bad, and the top one doesn't. It copied its neighbor to warn off hungry birds.

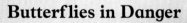

Butterflies in Danger
This homerus swallowtail butterfly is in danger from collectors. Many other butterflies are in danger because their jungle homes are being destroyed.

The caterpillars are covered with spines.

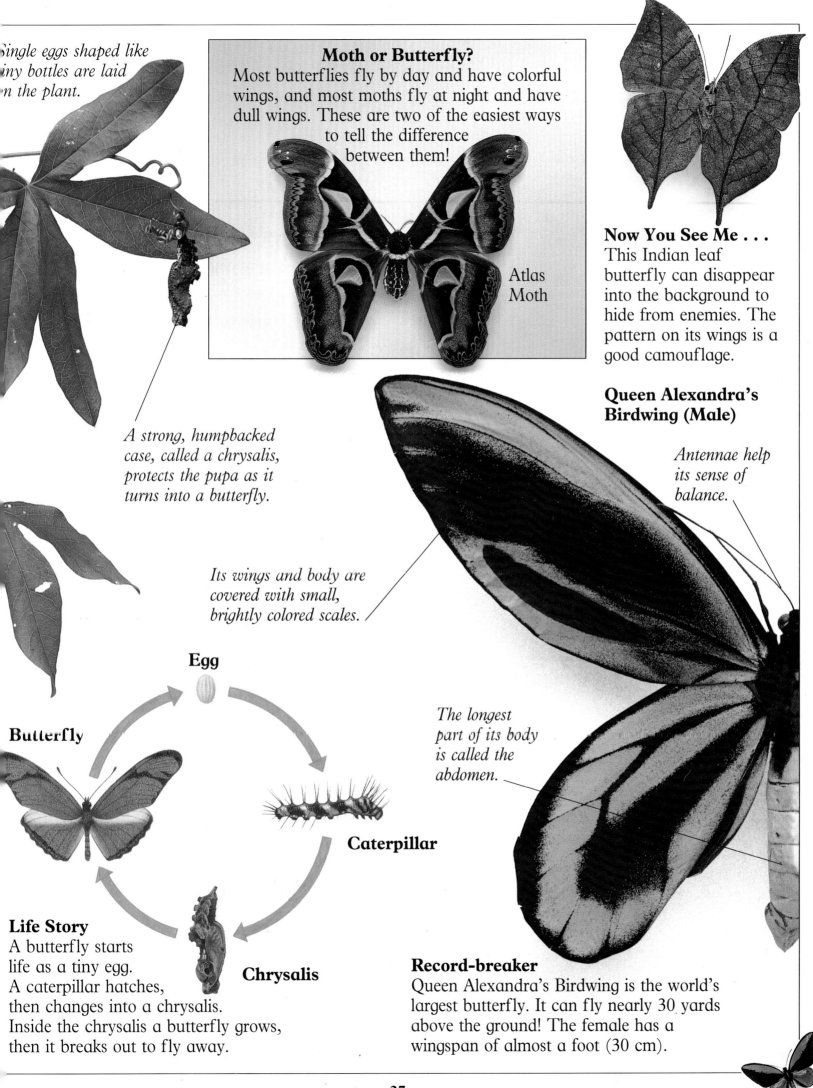

Single eggs shaped like tiny bottles are laid on the plant.

Moth or Butterfly?
Most butterflies fly by day and have colorful wings, and most moths fly at night and have dull wings. These are two of the easiest ways to tell the difference between them!

Atlas Moth

A strong, humpbacked case, called a chrysalis, protects the pupa as it turns into a butterfly.

Now You See Me . . .
This Indian leaf butterfly can disappear into the background to hide from enemies. The pattern on its wings is a good camouflage.

Queen Alexandra's Birdwing (Male)

Antennae help its sense of balance.

Its wings and body are covered with small, brightly colored scales.

Egg

Butterfly

The longest part of its body is called the abdomen.

Caterpillar

Chrysalis

Life Story
A butterfly starts life as a tiny egg. A caterpillar hatches, then changes into a chrysalis. Inside the chrysalis a butterfly grows, then it breaks out to fly away.

Record-breaker
Queen Alexandra's Birdwing is the world's largest butterfly. It can fly nearly 30 yards above the ground! The female has a wingspan of almost a foot (30 cm).

INSECTS

Do you know how many people there are in your family? Nobody knows how many different kinds of insects there are in the insect family. New species, or kinds, are found on most jungle expeditions. There may be thousands, perhaps even millions, of species yet to be discovered.

These ants do not eat the leaves. They carry them to their nest and eat the fungus that grows on the leaves.

Living Underground
Leaf-cutting ants carry leaves to their huge underground nest. As many as two and a half million ants live inside!

Ants can carry pieces of leaf that are more than twice their size.

Termite Tower
Some kinds of termites build nests like towers. The umbrella-shaped roofs keep the rain out.

Soldier termites defend the nest. They protect the other termites from danger.

Worker termites feed the soldier termites, because they cannot feed themselves.

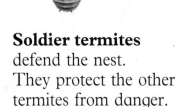

The queen termite lays eggs. The workers feed her because she is too big to move or leave the nest.

A small ant follows the worker ant, fighting off tiny phorid flies that try to lay their eggs on the worker's neck.

Going to Work
Two worker ants are cutting out a large chunk of leaf with their strong jaws.

3 2 1 Liftoff!
Beetles fly as well as crawl. They fold their wings under wing cases.

This jewel beetle may open and shut its wing cases a few times before take-off.

At last, the wing cases open wide to let the beetle stretch its wings and fly away.

Amazing Beetles

The African goliath beetle is the world's heaviest beetle. It weighs about three and a half ounces (100 g) and gets energy to fly from eating lots of fruit.

One of the world's smallest beetles, *Nasonella Fungi*, lives in the South American jungle. It could easily crawl through the eye of a needle!

Antenna

Eye

Thorax

Wing cases

Claw

(Actual size)

INSECT-EATERS

The number of insects living in the jungle is so huge, that some jungle animals can survive on a diet of insects alone. Anteaters and pangolins are well adapted to eating ants and termites. They break into hard nests using their strong claws, then catch the ants and termites with their long, sticky tongues. They have no teeth to chew with, so they swallow the insects whole!

African tree pangolin

Insect Hunter
A southern tamandua is a kind of anteater. It spends most of its life in the trees, searching for ants and termites at night.

When a southern tamandua pokes its snout into insect nests, it shoots out a long, sticky tongue to catch the escaping insects.

Dinnertime
This tree anteater has found a termite nest. It will smash it open with its strong arms and sharp claws.

Other Insect Hunters

Sloth bear

Moonrat

Dark patches of fur around a tamandua's neck look like a collar.

Southern tamandua

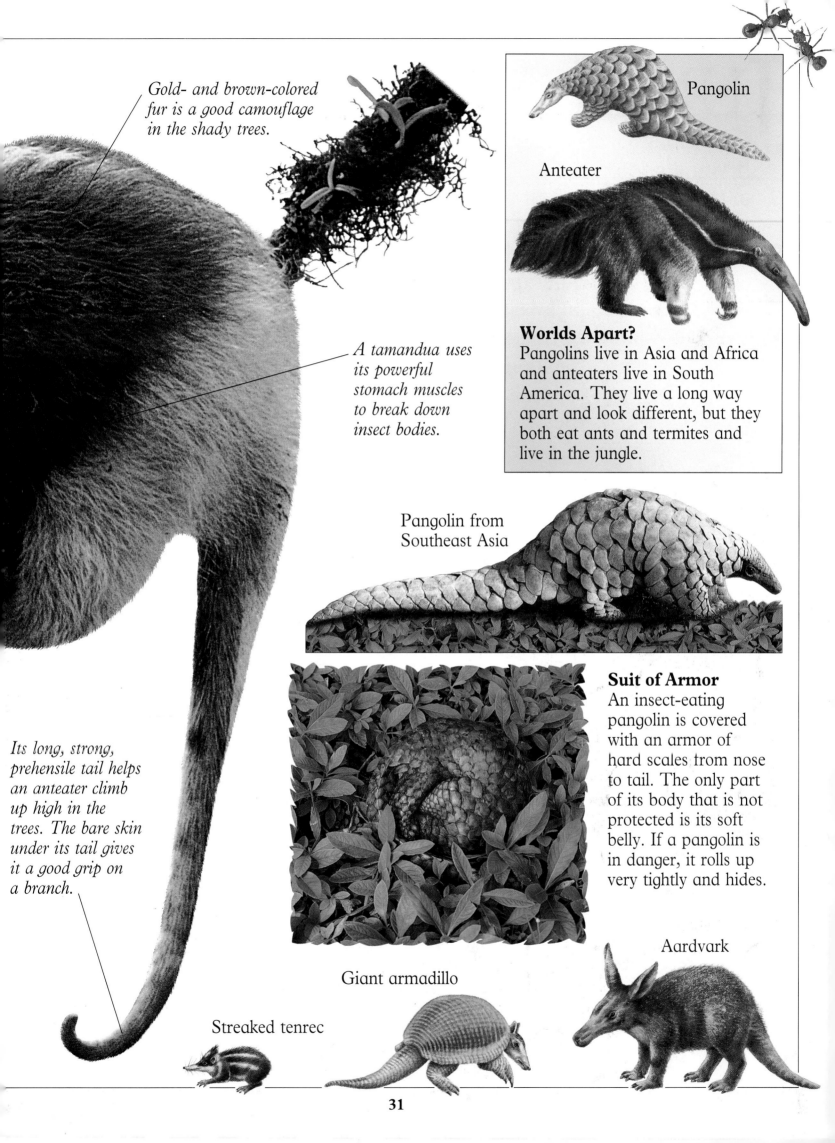

Gold- and brown-colored fur is a good camouflage in the shady trees.

A tamandua uses its powerful stomach muscles to break down insect bodies.

Pangolin

Anteater

Worlds Apart?
Pangolins live in Asia and Africa and anteaters live in South America. They live a long way apart and look different, but they both eat ants and termites and live in the jungle.

Pangolin from Southeast Asia

Its long, strong, prehensile tail helps an anteater climb up high in the trees. The bare skin under its tail gives it a good grip on a branch.

Suit of Armor
An insect-eating pangolin is covered with an armor of hard scales from nose to tail. The only part of its body that is not protected is its soft belly. If a pangolin is in danger, it rolls up very tightly and hides.

Aardvark

Giant armadillo

Streaked tenrec

JUNGLE GIANTS

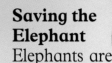

If you stand on the jungle floor and look up at the trees, you might suddenly feel very tiny. Trees tower above you like leafy skyscrapers. If you are quiet and still, you might be lucky enough to spy one of nature's giants looking for food nearby. Most big animals are more shy than they look, and will keep out of your way if they can.

Saving the Elephant
Elephants are hunted and killed for their ivory tusks. In 1990, most countries agreed to stop buying and selling ivory. Elephants are not hunted so much today, but the Asian elephant is still an endangered species.

Tremendous Tusks
Male elephants use their sharp tusks for fighting. The biggest Asian elephant tusks measured were nearly 6 feet (183 cm) long.

Elephants flap their ears to fan themselves in the hot jungle.

Elephants have poor eyesight, but they can smell and hear well.

The elephant reaches up with its trunk to grab leaves from jungle trees.

A deep rumble, made in the elephant's throat, is too low for humans to hear. But it can be heard by other elephants a long way away.

An elephant could pick up a thread from a polished floor with the tip of its trunk.

The trunk has more than 40,000 muscles in it – more than you have in your whole body.

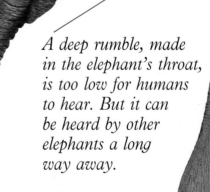

Some of the Jungle's Giants

The giant forest hog is the world's largest wild pig. Its body is 6 feet (1.8 m) long.

The Rafflesia Plant

The rafflesia plant has the world's widest flower. It is a yard across and its petals are nearly an inch (2½ cm) thick. It attracts flies because it smells like rotten meat. The flies then help to spread the rafflesia's pollen.

A Malayan tapir grows to be the size of a donkey.

Marathon Walker

Asian elephants walk a long way! Each herd has a territory of up to 300 square miles (777 km²). That's nearly five times the size of Washington, D.C.

The Sumatran rhinoceros often bulldozes small trees to reach the leaves.

A Brazilian tapir is the biggest hoofed animal in the South American jungle.

An elephant's skin can be as thick as an inch (2½ cm) on its back and on some parts of its head.

The goliath frog can grow to be the size of a small dog.

A bird-eating spider has a leg span of 10 inches (25 cm).

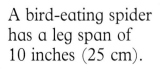

BIG CATS

Jungle cats are big and beautiful, but watch out – they can be dangerous! They prowl through the forest, hunting at night. They have big appetites, and often attack wild pigs and deer. They only attack people if they're very old, sick, or hungry.

Playtime
Just like pet kittens, the small cubs of big cats enjoy playing together.

Sneaky Leap
Have you ever seen a pet cat sneak up on a bird and pounce on it? Tigers creep toward their prey and crouch to the ground before the kill, just like pet cats.

Are Tigers Afraid of Water?
No way! Tigers are champion swimmers, and will catch fish, frogs, and turtles if they need to.

When angry, tigers twitch their tails.

The back legs have strong muscles and provide the power for leaping.

The tiger's orangy-red fur is lighter on its belly.

Disappearing Trick
Leopards are covered with black spots, which help them hide in shady jungle treetops.

Tiger

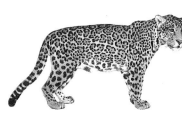

Leopard

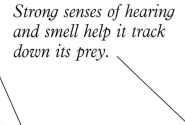

Its stripes make a tiger harder to see from a long way off.

Born blind, a tiger cub soon opens its eyes to see. Adult tigers are usually nocturnal. That means they are active after dark.

Strong senses of hearing and smell help it track down its prey.

Jaguar

Ocelot

Clouded leopard

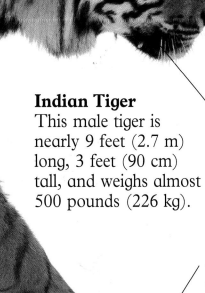

Indian Tiger
This male tiger is nearly 9 feet (2.7 m) long, 3 feet (90 cm) tall, and weighs almost 500 pounds (226 kg).

It kills by biting at its prey's neck and throat with its sharp teeth.

Its claws come out from sheaths when a tiger climbs a tree or pounces on its prey.

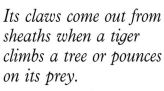

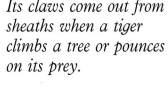

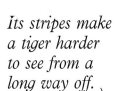

35

SNAKES

Some of the world's most dangerous snakes live in the jungle, but most will stay out of your way if you don't bother them. Snakes often hide up in the trees, where they wait to catch the birds and mammals that live up there, too. Snakes are cold-blooded reptiles, which means they need food to grow, but not to keep warm and active. One meal can keep them going for days!

First Sign of Life
Most snakes hatch from eggs, like this bushmaster snake from South America.

Easy Does It
When they hatch, baby snakes peek out to take a first look at the outside world.

Super Snake
The anaconda is the world's heaviest snake. A 26-foot (8 m) long anaconda weighs about 500 pounds (227 kg)! Anacondas can crush even caimans to death and swallow them.

Wear and Tear
A snake's skin does not last forever. About four times a year, this Pope's pit viper rubs its mouth against something rough to loosen the skin. Then out it wriggles. A brand new skin has grown underneath the old one.

Here I Come!
When a snake hatches, it is amazing to see how such a long body could have fit into such a small egg.

Its beady eyes face forward, so that it can focus on things in the distance.

Vine Snake
The vine snake hunts small birds and lizards in the jungle trees of Africa. Much of its day is spent hanging very still in the branches. When it does move, it goes off in slow motion.

It can grow to be up to two yards (2 m) long. The end of its tail is thinner than your finger.

Hundreds of hard scales cover its body. They fit together like floor tiles.

A long, thin green body makes the snake hard to see among the creepers and vines.

Spot the Snake
Hidden in these leaves is an African gaboon viper. It lurks on the jungle floor, waiting to poison its prey with its long, deadly fangs. The snake is very well camouflaged by the pattern on its skin.

The gaboon viper's head and body are very hard to see.

LIZARDS

Gold skink

Lizards have roamed the Earth for millions of years and look like smaller versions of dinosaurs. Chameleons and other lizards are cold-blooded reptiles, so their body temperature goes up and down with the heat. They use tricks to keep their temperature level, such as storing up heat from the middle of the day to keep them warm in the cool of the night.

Heads Up!
If you walk through the South American jungle, watch out for frightened iguanas dropping down from the branches above you!

Madagascan Chameleon

Day gecko

A chameleon winds up its tail to make a heavy weight. It uses the weight to balance itself when it is sitting on a branch.

Solomon Island skink

All Change!

On a hot, sunny day, you might put on a brightly colored T-shirt. Chameleons turn a lighter color as the cells in their skin get smaller with the heat and light.

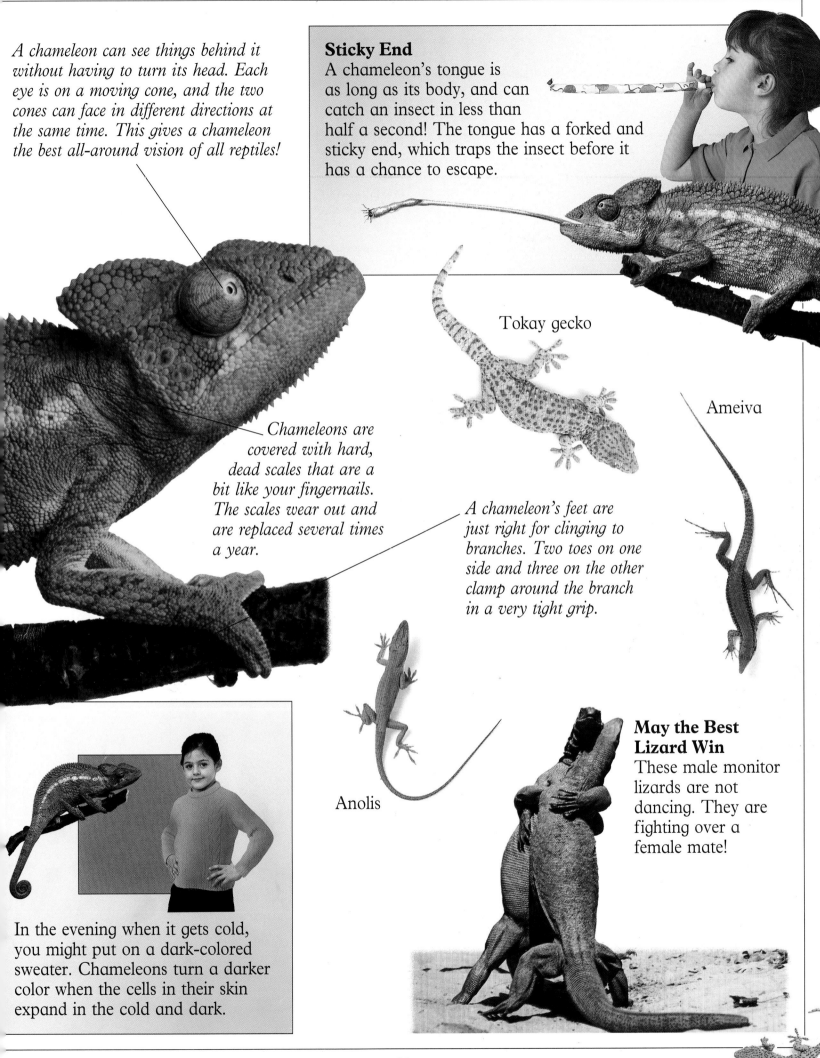

A chameleon can see things behind it without having to turn its head. Each eye is on a moving cone, and the two cones can face in different directions at the same time. This gives a chameleon the best all-around vision of all reptiles!

Sticky End
A chameleon's tongue is as long as its body, and can catch an insect in less than half a second! The tongue has a forked and sticky end, which traps the insect before it has a chance to escape.

Tokay gecko

Ameiva

Chameleons are covered with hard, dead scales that are a bit like your fingernails. The scales wear out and are replaced several times a year.

A chameleon's feet are just right for clinging to branches. Two toes on one side and three on the other clamp around the branch in a very tight grip.

Anolis

May the Best Lizard Win
These male monitor lizards are not dancing. They are fighting over a female mate!

In the evening when it gets cold, you might put on a dark-colored sweater. Chameleons turn a darker color when the cells in their skin expand in the cold and dark.

CROCODILES

Crocodiles are the great hunters of jungle rivers. They eat fish, birds, mammals – and sometimes people, too! They float almost hidden by the water, like dark, knobby logs, watching and waiting for their next meal. Many only eat once a week, but when they do, they feast!

Some crocodiles can stand upright on their strong tail and "tail walk."

Scales make good armor against a crocodile's enemies.

Its stomach is full of stones. A crocodile can't chew, so it swallows stones to mash up its food. The weight of the stones may also keep the crocodile low in the water.

Crocodiles can run faster than people can, even with such short legs!

Super Swimmer
To swim, a crocodile swishes hard with its tail. It keeps its legs close to its sides.

Crocodile Crisis

People kill crocodiles for their skin, which is used to make watch straps, handbags, and shoes. The Chinese alligator, the black caiman, and many other types of crocodiles are now nearly extinct – there are hardly any of them left alive.

The Crocodilian Family

The world's largest and most dangerous reptiles are in the crocodilian family.

Crocodile

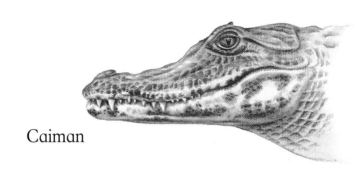

Caiman

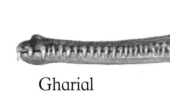

Gharial

Crocodiles have see-through, waterproof eyelids.

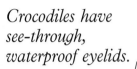

A hot crocodile opens its mouth, and the air helps it cool down.

Nile Crocodile

A Nile crocodile can grow up to 16 feet (4.8 m) long.

Crybaby

Crocodiles hatch from eggs. As they break out of their shells, they squeak loudly to attract their mother's attention.

Tooth Trouble

Humans have two sets of teeth in a lifetime, but crocodiles grow new teeth every time their old ones wear down. They can be longer than your fingers!

FISH

More kinds of fish swim in South America's Amazon River than in any other river in the world. Around 3,000 species hunt alone or in huge groups, eating anything from seeds to small crocodiles. The fish are as different from each other as are the animals in the jungle above them.

Piranha skull

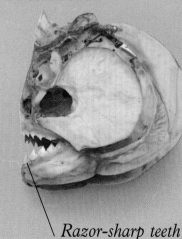

Razor-sharp teeth

Killer Fish
The red piranhas of the Amazon are the most dangerous fish in the world. They attack in groups of up to 1,000 fish, and can strip a large animal to the bone in just a few minutes.

The Flooded Forest
It rains so heavily in some parts of the South American jungle that the Amazon River floods for about half the year. An area of jungle larger than England is flooded.

Amazon Fish
The Amazon River is full of a huge number of fish of all shapes and sizes. Some are meat-eaters, while others are strictly vegetarian.

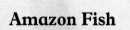

Neon tetras are only 1½ inches (4 cm) long.

At 8 feet (2.5 m) long, the pirarucu is one of the world's largest river fish.

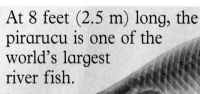

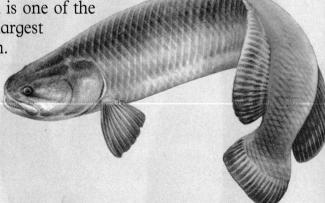

Dad's the Word

Arowana fish eggs are kept safe inside the father's mouth until they hatch. A fully grown arowana is one of the largest insect-eating fish in the world. It can grow to be a yard long.

The archer fish's big eyes help it judge how high it needs to jump to snap up a spider.

Jump to It!

The archer fish swims in the jungle rivers of Southeast Asia. If it is very hungry, it will jump out of the water to grab an insect from a leaf. Usually it spits jets of water at an insect to knock it off its perch.

It can leap 1 foot (30 cm) out of the water.

Fruity Smell

This tambaqui can smell when rubber trees are about to drop their seeds. It swims up to the surface and snatches the seeds as they fall. Many jungle fish eat fruit and spread the seeds through their droppings.

The pacu is a vegetarian piranha.

The arowana can leap nearly 4 feet (1.2 m) out of the river to snap up insects.

RIVER SWIMMERS

Jungle rivers are swimming with life. Turtles sit on riverbeds waiting to gulp down fish, while river dolphins and manatees cruise along in the water above them. Playful giant otters and families of capybaras splash in and out of the river, while jungle insects of all shapes and sizes live by the riverbank.

Giant water bugs

Unlike most turtles, this creature's head, neck, and feet don't fit inside its shell.

Water World
Many jungle insects love warm, damp places. Some, such as the giant water bug, snap up fish and frogs. Others, like the leech, suck blood.

Water scorpion

Leeches

Back swimmers

It can see well under water.

The turtle raises its neck out of the water to breathe.

Snake-necked Turtle
The snake-necked turtle sits on the jungle riverbeds of Southeast Asia. An adult turtle is about a foot (30 cm) long, and its neck is as long as its body.

This turtle eats fish, frogs, and insects. It crushes them in its hard, bony mouth because it doesn't have teeth to chew with.

Webbed feet help it swim fast to escape from enemies.

Amazing Jungle Swimmers

Guinea Pig Giant
The capybara is the world's biggest rodent – about five times bigger than a guinea pig! Strong, webbed feet make it a good swimmer. Its teeth never stop growing, but it munches plants to grind them down.

A manatee can be about the length of its relative, the Asian elephant.

River dolphins have at least 100 teeth!

The giant otter can grow to be more than 7 feet (2.1 m) long.

The matamata turtle's incredible disguise hides it within its riverbed home.

Underwater Baby
This manatee is born under water and swims in jungle rivers all its life. It can hold its breath for 16 minutes before swimming up to the surface of the water to snatch a gulp of air.

South American river turtles swim in large groups to find good nesting places.

Woolly
spider
monkey

JUNGLES IN DANGER

St. Vincent
parrot

Jungles are the richest habitats in the world. They are home to many people, as well as animals and plants. All the world's jungles could be destroyed in your lifetime, because they are being cut down for wood or burned to make room for farms and ranches. The animals on these pages are just some of the species in danger because their jungle homes are disappearing.

Up in Smoke
Areas of jungle where the land is needed for farming are often cut down and burned. The smoke from this burning jungle in South America can be seen from outer space.

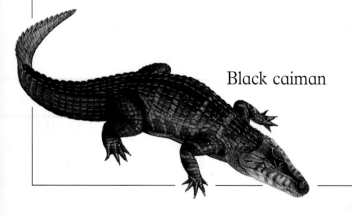

Black caiman

Javan rhinoceros

Tube-nosed
fruit bat

Rufous-breasted
hermit hummingbird

Sri Lankan
rose butterfly

Timber!
The wood from
some jungle trees,
such as teak and
mahogany, is used
to make furniture.

Seeds of Hope
An area of jungle the size of 40 football
fields disappears every minute, but some
people are trying hard to replace the trees.
This conservation worker collects seeds of
trees in the South American jungle,
so that they can be planted.

We Need Plants
Many jungle plants could become
extinct before people discover
how useful they are. The black
bean tree was in danger from
logging, but doctors have now
found out that the bean could be
useful in finding a cure for AIDS.

Black bean pod

Mountain
gorilla

Malayan tapir

Jaguar

GLOSSARY

Abdomen The soft belly of an insect.

Antennae A pair of feelers on the head of an insect, used to feel or taste.

Camouflage The color patterns or body shapes that help hide an animal's body in its surroundings.

Cells Living units that make up all living things.

Chemical A substance that is used in, or results from, a scientific reaction.

Chrysalis A stage in the life of an insect, during which a young insect turns into an adult. Pupa is another name for chrysalis.

Cold-blooded The temperature of a cold-blooded animal goes up and down with the temperature of its surroundings.

Conservation Preservation and protection of species and natural resources.

Crocodilian Family of reptiles, including crocodiles, alligators, and caimans.

Endangered Animals or plants that are in danger of dying out, or becoming extinct.

Extinct A word to describe a species that has died out.

Fang A long, pointed tooth. Snakes' fangs are often hollow and filled with poison.

Fungus A plant, such as mold, that grows and spreads quickly, without roots, stems, or leaves.

Habitat The place where a plant or animal lives, for example, a jungle or a desert.

Ivory Elephant tusks are made of this hard, smooth material.

Logging Cutting down trees is called logging.

Mammal All mammals are warm-blooded, which means that their body temperature stays the same, however hot or cold their surroundings are. Mammals breathe air and feed their babies milk.

Nectar The sweet liquid that is hidden deep inside a flower.

Nocturnal Animals that sleep during the day and stay awake at night.

Opposable Like most primates, you have an opposable thumb. This means you can move it easily across the palm of your hand.

Pollen Fine powder inside the flowers of seed-making plants.

Pollination The transfer of pollen from the male to the female part of a flower. New seeds are made so that new plants can grow.

Prehensile tail A tail that can wind around branches in a tight grip.

Prey An animal that is caught and eaten by another animal.

Primates Humans, monkeys, and apes are included in the group of animals called primates. Primates are usually intelligent, with flexible hands and good eyesight.

Reptile A cold-blooded animal that is covered with scales. Reptiles breathe air and most hatch from eggs.

Rodent The family of mammals that includes guinea pigs, rats, and mice. Rodents are always gnawing food or other things to grind down their teeth.

Roost To rest or sleep, often on a branch. Fruit bats roost in trees.

Scales Small, hard plates that cover the bodies of some animals.

Species A type of animal or plant. Any male and female member of the same species can breed together.

Territory An area of land that an animal, or group of animals, uses and defends against other animals.

Thorax The middle part of an insect's body, carrying the legs and wings.

Tusk A long, pointed tooth made of ivory.

Vegetarian An animal that feeds only on plants.

Wing case The hard shell of a beetle that protects the delicate wings underneath.

Wingspan The distance between two wing tips.

Acknowledgments

Photography: Steve Bartholomew, Tina Chambers, Steve Gorton, Colin Keates ABIPP, Tim Ridley, James Stevenson; **Illustrations:** Sandra Doyle, Roy Flooks, Mick Gillah, Mick Loates, Malcolm McGregor; **Models:** Donks Models; **Thanks to:** H. Samuel Ltd.; London Butterfly House, Syon Park; Royal Botanical Gardens, Kew; The Natural History Museum, London; Truly Scrumptious Child Model Agency.

INDEX